This Journal Belongs to:

_____

_____

_____

Great works are performed not by
strength but by perseverance.
— Samuel Johnson

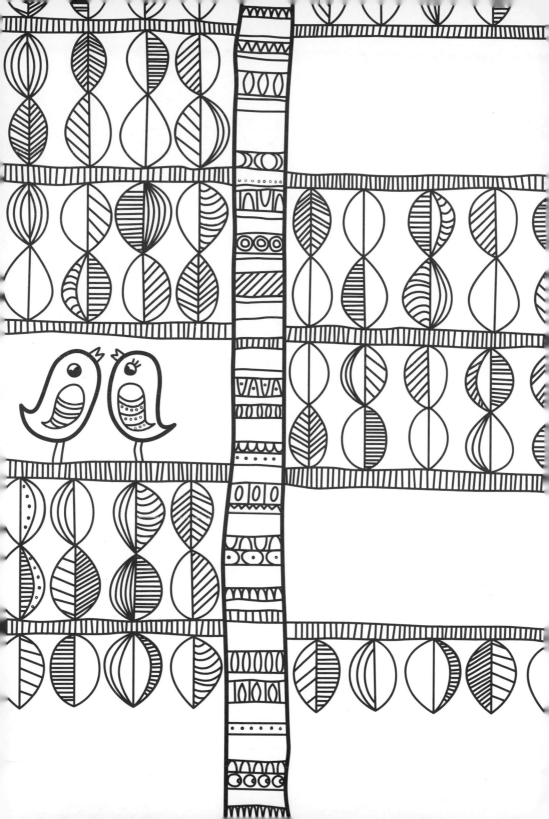

Life is beautiful.

I will be grateful for this day.

With each sunrise, we start anew.

You only live once. If you do it right, once is enough.

_____

_____

_____

_____

_____

_____

_____

_____

_____

_____

_____

_____

_____

_____

_____

_____

_____

_____

_____

_____

_____

_____

Work hard to have a good result.

Happiness is not a destination. It's a way of life.

_____

_____

_____

_____

_____

_____

_____

_____

_____

_____

_____

_____

_____

_____

_____

_____

_____

_____

_____

_____

May all paths lead to happiness,
and may all your dreams come true.

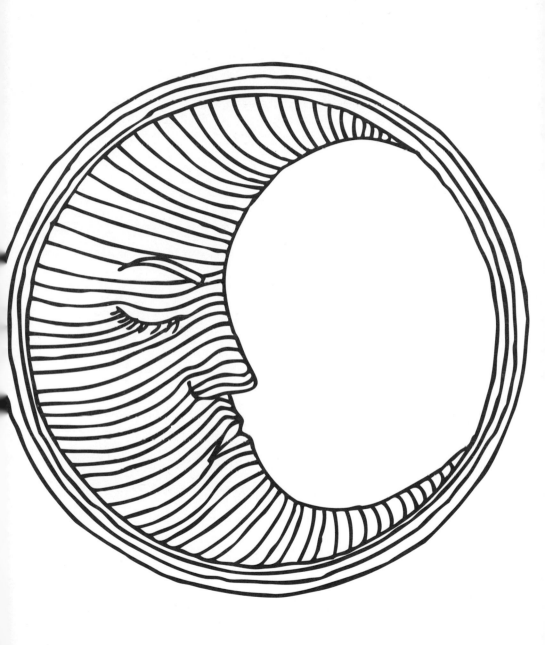

Laugh every day.

You make me happy when skies are gray.

Positive vibes only.

_____
_____
_____
_____
_____
_____
_____
_____
_____
_____
_____
_____
_____
_____
_____
_____
_____
_____
_____
_____
_____
_____
_____
_____

Believe in yourself.

Believe you can, and you're halfway there.

_____

_____

_____

_____

_____

_____

_____

_____

_____

_____

_____

_____

_____

_____

_____

_____

_____

_____

_____

_____

_____

_____

SMILE

One changes from day to day . . .
every few years one becomes a new being.
— George Sand

It just wouldn't be a picnic without the ants.

It's what's inside that counts.

Collect memories, not things.

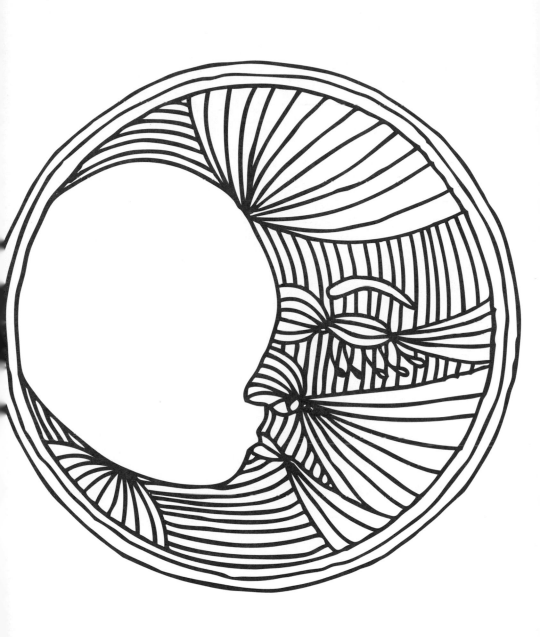

The spiritual eyesight improves as
the physical eyesight declines.
— Plato

Don't wait for your ship
to come in. Swim out to it.

LIFE ·IS· NOT about FINDING yourself LIFE IS about CREATING YOURSELF

Live in the sunshine,
swim the sea, drink the wild air.
— Ralph Waldo Emerson

Follow your heart.

LIFE IS BEAUTIFUL

The start of each day is a promise of love.

Do small things with great love.

Life is hard by the yard; by the inch, it's a cinch.

Let your faith be bigger than your fear.

Love never fails.
— I Corinthians 13:8

Live. Laugh. Love.

Dream big dreams.

Love bears all things, believes all things,
hopes all things, endures all things.

Enjoy the little things.

Little by little does the trick.
— Aesop

BE
YOURSELF
everyone
ELSE IS
ALREADY
taken

Keep Calm and Color

Plant your feet firmly but let your heart have wings.

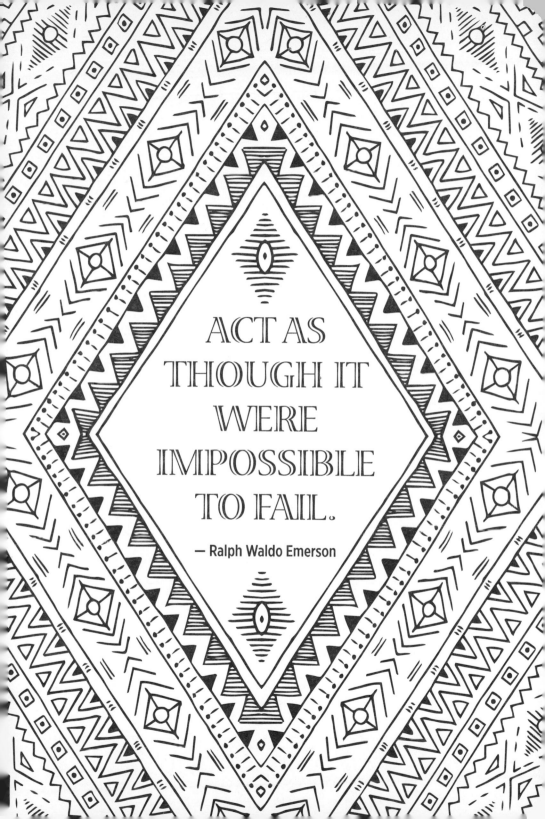

ACT AS THOUGH IT WERE IMPOSSIBLE TO FAIL.

— Ralph Waldo Emerson

Laughter is the best gift a friend can give.

_____

_____

_____

_____

_____

_____

_____

_____

_____

_____

_____

_____

_____

_____

_____

_____

_____

_____

_____

_____

_____

_____

_____

When life gives you lemons, make margaritas.

Therefore encourage one another and build one another up.
— Thessalonians 5:11

_____

_____

_____

_____

_____

_____

_____

_____

_____

_____

_____

_____

_____

_____

_____

_____

_____

_____

_____
_____
_____
_____
_____
_____
_____
_____
_____
_____
_____
_____
_____
_____
_____
_____
_____
_____
_____
_____
_____
_____
_____

Life isn't about waiting for the storm to pass;
it's about learning to dance in the rain.

I praise you because I am fearfully and wonderfully made.
— Psalm 139:14

_____
_____
_____
_____
_____
_____
_____
_____
_____
_____
_____
_____
_____
_____
_____
_____
_____
_____
_____

So now faith, hope and love abide . . .
but the greatest of these is love.
— I Corinthians 13:13

_____

_____

_____

_____

_____

_____

_____

_____

_____

_____

_____

_____

_____

_____

_____

_____

_____

_____

_____

_____

_____

_____

_____

Blessed are the happiness makers.